MILITARY JOBS

MARINES

What It takes to Join the Elite

ALEXANDER STILWELL

Cavendish
Square

New York

Published in 2015 by Cavendish Square Publishing, LLC
243 5th Avenue, Suite 136, New York, NY 10016

First edition

Website: cavendishsq.com

This publication represents the opinions and views of the author based on his or her personal experiences, knowledge, and research. The information in this book serves as a general guide only. The author and publisher have used their best efforts in preparing this book and disclaim liability rising directly or indirectly from the use and application of this book.

CPSIA compliance information: Batch #WW15CSQ.

All websites were available and accurate when this book was sent to press.

Library of Congress Cataloging-in-Publication Data

Stillwell, Alexander.
 Marines : what it takes to join the elite / Alexander Stilwell.
     pages cm. — (Military jobs)
 Includes index.
 ISBN 978-1-50260-164-3 (hardcover) ISBN 978-1-50260-168-1 (ebook)
 1. United States. Marine Corps. 2. Marines—Training of—United States. I. Title.

 VE23.S745 2014
 359.9'602373—dc23

                        2014026753

For Brown Bear Books Ltd:
Editorial Director: Lindsey Lowe
Managing Editor: Tim Cooke
Children's Publisher: Anne O'Daly
Design Manager: Keith Davis
Designer: Lynne Lennon
Picture Manager: Sophie Mortimer

Picture Credits:
T=Top, C=Center, B=Bottom, L=Left, R=Right

Front Cover : FC All images Library of Congress
All images © Library of Congress, except; 10, © Bettmann/Corbis; 30, © Shutterstock.

Brown Bear Books has made every attempt to contact the copyright holder.
If you have any information please contact licensing@brownbearbooks.co.uk.

We believe the extracts included in this book to be material in the public domain.
Anyone having any further information should contact licensing@brownbearbooks.co.uk.

Manufactured in the United States of America

CONTENTS

INTRODUCTION

The United States Marine Corps (USMC) is an elite force of 177,000 trained fighters. It can fight from land, sea, and air simultaneously, depending on the mission.

Marines are trained to fight in all terrains from the Arctic and the high mountains to deserts and jungles. The Marine Corps is relatively small in comparison with other U.S. armed services, but it makes up for its size through mobility and efficiency.

The Marine Corps includes a number of specialist arms, including the 1st Reconnaissance Battalion 1st Marine Division, better known as Marine Recon. This special operations unit carries out reconnaissance in advance of Marine landings. The Marines also have a Scout Sniper Unit, which combines reconnaissance and sniper roles. The Corps incorporates the United States Marine Corps Forces Special Operations Command (MARSOC). This conducts direct action, special reconnaissance, foreign internal defense, counterterrorism and information operations.

A U.S. Marine Corps lance corporal displays the Marine Corps flag during an evening parade.

⏵⏵ HISTORY

The Marine Corps is older than the United States itself. It was founded on November 10, 1775, by the Continental Congress. Its role was to seize naval bases in support of naval campaigns.

Marines come ashore in the Bahamas in March 1777, when they made their first amphibious assault to capture the British-held port of Nassau.

The Marines still have a close link with amphibious operations, but they also fight more conventional land battles.

The 20th Century

In World War I (1914–1918), the U.S. Marines established a reputation as tough fighters. They fought in a famous action

at Belleau Wood on the Western Front, where they halted the German advance. In World War II (1939–1945), they played a leading role in many battles against Japan in the Pacific Ocean. They made amphibious landings on islands such as Guadalcanal, Tarawa, and Iwo Jima.

IN ACTION

The Marines have been at the forefront of U.S. wars in the twenty-first century. Marines were the first conventional forces to enter Afghanistan as part of Operation Enduring Freedom in 2001. They were also part of the spearhead that led the coalition invasion of Iraq in 2003.

U.S. Marines raise the Stars and Stripes on Iwo Jima in February 1945, during the Pacific War against Japan.

After World War II

A provisional Marine force was operational in the Korean War (1950–1953) and the Marines fought in the Vietnam War (1965–1975). They were involved in fighting the Viet Cong guerrillas who waged a covert war against U.S. forces. Marines also deployed in Operation Desert Shield in the Gulf War of 1990, and later in the global War on Terror.

⟫ WHAT IT TAKES

The Marines accept both male and female recruits—but everyone has to be prepared to say goodbye to their civilian self and be re-created as a self-assured and capable warrior.

U.S. Marine colonels salute during a change of command ceremony for Headquarters Battalion, 1st Marine Division.

Before you are even considered for basic training in the U.S. Marine Corps, you have to pass the Initial Strength Test (IST). This consists of:
- Pull-ups on a bar: minimum of two to pass.
- Crunches: forty-four in two minutes (to

 Marines carry 2nd Marine Battalion flags during a ceremony. The Marines are proud of their traditions.

perform a crunch, lie on your back with arms crossed and knees raised. Raise your upper body to touch your knees then return to the starting position).
• Timed run: Candidates must complete a 1.5-mile (2.4-km) run in under 13 minutes and 30 seconds if male, or under 15 minutes if female.

Welcome, Marine

After surviving the initial strength test, candidates must then survive a verbal onslaught from their drill instructors throughout their training. But if they can pass these tests, candidates are admitted into the Marine Corps. They are almost immediately issued with a rifle—they are now a U.S. Marine.

EYEWITNESS

"You can be in the Navy. You can be in the Air Force. And you can be in the Army. But, you ARE a Marine."
—**S.F. Tomajczyk,**
"To Be a U.S. Marine"

▶▶ BOOT CAMP

A new recruit's first experience of the Marine Corps comes at Boot Camp. It's as tough as its name suggests. Drill instructors scream and shout at the recruits to simulate the stress of war.

Boot Camp lasts twelve weeks at either Parris Island, South Carolina, or San Diego, California. In both places the new recruits, or poolees, are following a long tradition.

The parade grounds are painted with yellow footprints to show exactly where to stand. The footprints underline the discipline required to be a Marine. But they are also a reminder that the poolees have to live up to the glories of past Marines in whose footsteps they are following.

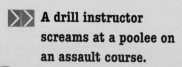
▶▶ **A drill instructor screams at a poolee on an assault course.**

The poolees learn drill and marksmanship. They take courses to improve their confidence and teamwork. Close-quarter combat in martial arts is also a major part of the course.

Into the Crucible

Boot Camp ends with a test known as the Crucible. For fifty-four hours, the poolees get little food or sleep while facing a series of exercises designed to test their fitness and their skills at markmanship and martial arts. Thanks to the drill instructors, about ninety percent of poolees make it through Boot Camp to become Marines.

EYEWITNESS

"For many recruits, pugil stick training is the most intense physical combat they have ever experienced. They have to learn to act despite fear in order to outmaneuver and overpower an opponent."

—U.S. Marine Corps, Recruit Training

 A poolee struggles as he crawls beneath barbed wire carrying his rifle at the ready.

►► SCHOOL OF INFANTRY

At the end of Boot Camp, recruits receive their prized Marine badge. They head to the School of Infantry (SOI) to learn the skills they need to be an effective member of a Marine combat unit.

There are two separate camps: SOI East in North Carolina and SOI West in California. They both offer the standard Infantry Training Battalion and the Marine Combat Training Battalion, which is a shorter course for non-infantry Marines who are specialists in support roles.

A combat instructor directs students during a live-fire mortar exercise.

Infantry Training Battalion

This course lasts fifty-nine days. Recruits improve their marksmanship, but they also learn patrol skills, reconnaissance, land navigation, convoy operations, and urban operations (UO). At the same time they continue to improve their physical fitness and practice martial arts.

Marine Combat Training Battalion

This course lasts twenty-nine days. It teaches combat skills to Marines who are specialists rather than infantry. Training includes combat operations, fire-team assaults, land navigation, patrolling, and UO.

 Infantry trainees with M16A4 rifles receive instruction before part of a marksmanship course.

EYEWITNESS

"This is my rifle. There are many like it, but this one is mine. My rifle is my best friend. It is my life. I must master it as I master my life. My rifle, without me, is useless. Without my rifle, I am useless. I must fire my rifle true. I must shoot straighter than any enemy who is trying to kill me. I must shoot him before he shoots me. I will."

—Major-General William H. Rupertus, USMC, "This Is My Rifle"

▷▷ OFFICER CANDIDATE SCHOOL

**Only the best Marines get to be officers.
They have to know more than their men about
navigation and tactics. They have to be fitter, too.
Marine officers always lead from the front.**

Officer Candidate School (OCS) is designed to identify those who have the qualities needed to make the grade. The ten-week course is focused on one idea: leadership. Candidates have to show not only that they have leadership qualities but also that those qualities remain constant in a stressful environment.

Learning Leadership

The course assesses different aspects of what it takes to be a good leader. The Leadership Reaction Course, for example, tests problem-solving skills.

▷▷ **An OCS instructor makes a barbed
wire obstacle for a field exercise.**

 Students at OCS are under constant, close-range pressure from drill instructors.

Whatever the task, assessors study whether candidates have the ability to motivate their men and make good decisions even when they are exhausted by physical exertion and lack of sleep. The assessors want to identify leaders with determination and stamina.

Physical Fitness

Throughout their leadership training, OCS continues to put potential officers through intense physical training to raise their fitness levels. The exercises include 12-mile (19-km) hikes in full gear, a "Tarzan" rope course, and a combat simulation course.

EYEWITNESS

"Set the standards for your Marines by personal example. The Marines in your unit all watch your appearance, attitude, physical fitness and personal example. If your personal standards are high, then you can rightly demand the same of your Marines."

—U.S. Marine Corps

⟫ THE BASIC SCHOOL

Newly commissioned Marine officers head for The Basic School, which is another 26-week course. They try to live up to the Five Horizontal Themes that define the qualities a USMC officer needs.

According to the Five Horizontal Themes, a USMC officer must be:

General James F. Amos, commandant of the Marines Corps, visits students at the Basic School in 2014.

- A man or woman of exemplary character.
- Devoted to leading Marines 24/7.
- Able to decide, communicate, and act in the fog of war.

- A warfighter who embraces the Corps' warrior ethos.
- Mentally strong and physically tough.

Basic Principles

All Marine officers at the Basic School learn to apply eleven basic leadership principles:

1) Be technically and tactically proficient.
2) Know yourself and seek self-improvement.
3) Know your Marines and look after their welfare.

 Marines at the Basic School enter an abandoned building during an urban warfare exercise.

4) Keep your Marines informed.
5) Set the example.
6) Ensure the task is understood, supervised, and accomplished.
7) Train your Marines as a team.
8) Make sound and timely decisions.
9) Develop a sense of responsibility in your subordinates.
10) Employ your unit in accordance with its capabilities.
11) Seek responsibility and take responsibility for your actions.

▶▶ MARINE EXPEDITIONARY FORCE

Marines are trained to go into action with all the equipment and people they might need to create a complete fighting force.

Part of a Marine Expeditionary Unit comes ashore during a military exercise in 2005.

The largest organizational unit is the Marine Expeditionary Force (MEF), which includes between 46,000 and 90,000 Marines. It includes a ground combat element, an aircraft wing, and logistics and support groups.

 Marines fire an M-777 howitzer during an exercise. They travel with their own artillery support.

Expeditionary Brigade

The Marine Expeditionary Brigade (MEB) is smaller than an MEF, but includes the same ground and air elements. It is usually only between 4,000 and 16,000 Marines strong, however.

Expeditionary Unit

This smaller task force consists of about 2,200 Marines, a helicopter squadron, and a combat logistics battalion. It is highly mobile and is normally deployed close to the front line.

EYEWITNESS

"Overseas presence is the visible posture of U.S. forces and infrastructure strategically positioned forward, in or near key regions... Deployed forces promote security and stability, prevent conflict, give substance to our security commitments and ensure our continued success."

—Leatherneck Magazine

MARINE SCOUT SNIPER

The Marine Corps take a unique approach to sniping. It uses snipers to shoot at designated targets, but also uses them for reconnaissance and surveillance work.

A Marine scout sniper unloads his weapon during a training course.

A Marine Scout Sniper is part of a Scout Sniper Platoon, but usually works as part of a two-man team made up of a spotter and a sniper. The spotter

helps identify targets, works out the range, and calculates how wind conditions might affect the trajectory of the bullet. The sniper's job is to get covertly into position to fire at a designated target, which might be enemy personnel or equipment. Snipers use heavy caliber sniper rifles to disable vehicles or signaling equipment.

Defensive Firearms

Spotters are usually armed with an automatic rifle such as an M16 to provide defense for the sniper team. The sniper will use a specialist rifle, such as the M40.

EYEWITNESS

"There are two primary missions of Marine Scout Snipers: recon and targeted strikes on enemy personnel and equipment. They can be more devastating on enemy forces than a plane full of bombs."

—Geoffrey Ingersoll, editor, Marine Corps Times

A spotter looks on as a sniper prepares to take a long-range shot on an exercise in Djibouti, Africa.

>> MARINE CRITICAL SKILLS OPERATOR

Critical Skills Operators (CSOs) are the Marines' own special forces. These Marines have a wide range of skills and are highly adaptable, so they can make quick decisions in fast-moving situtations.

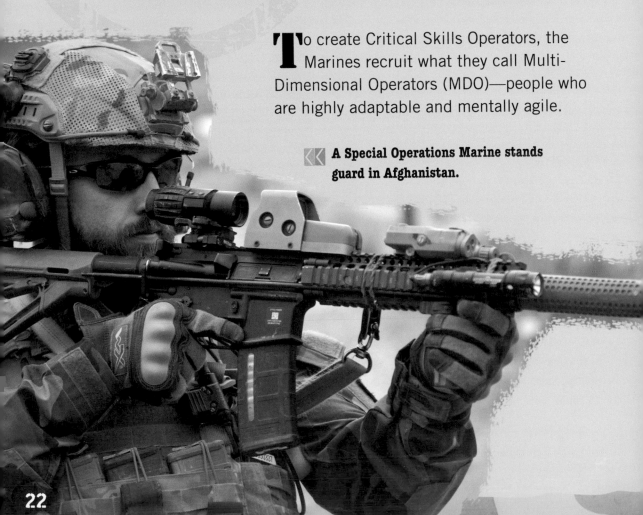

To create Critical Skills Operators, the Marines recruit what they call Multi-Dimensional Operators (MDO)—people who are highly adaptable and mentally agile.

《《 A Special Operations Marine stands guard in Afghanistan.

PERRES Course

Critical Skills Operators follow a course especially developed for the Marines called Performance and Resiliency (PERRES). This course sets out to create Marines who are not just physically fit but who also have the spiritual strength to cope with the stress of modern warfare. It takes a holistic approach to wellness. CSOs work with physical therapists, psychologists, and chaplains to learn how best to avoid physical injury and mental anxiety.

EYEWITNESS

"Seventy-five to ninety-five percent of our warriors and their families experience long-term growth, family pride, enhanced self-esteem, strength development from stress inoculation and many other benefits from their service, acceptance of risk, and personal sacrifices."

—Dr. Carroll Greene, MARSOC Psychologist

Members of a Marine Special Operations Regiment on exercise clear an industrial facility.

MARINE FORCE RECON

Force Reconnaissance, or Force Recon, undertake reconnaissance and Direct Action (DA) missions in enemy territory. They have one of the most dangerous roles in the whole USMC.

Force Recon Marines share many of the same skills as the U.S. Navy special forces, the SEALs. They are trained to parachute into enemy territory from airplanes or to be dropped from helicopters or from submarines. They are also trained to board and search ships for illegal arms, drugs, or other cargoes.

Force Recon Marines come ashore on a beach as part of an exercise in covert landings.

 Marines of the 3rd Reconaissance Battalion pause during a patrol at the Jungle Warfare School in Okinawa, Japan.

Intelligence Gathering

Force Recon's main task is to gather intelligence before an assault and to carry out preparatory operations to enable a Marine Expeditionary Force to make a successful landing. Force Recon Marines carry out patrols deep behind enemy lines. They are also expert in small-scale raids on enemy gun emplacements or communications facilities.

EYEWITNESS

"Conquering all obstacles, both large and small, I shall never quit. To quit, to surrender, to give up is to fail. To be a Recon Marine is to surpass failure; to overcome, to adapl, and to do whatever it takes to complete the mission. On the battlefield, as in all areas of life, I shall stand tall above the competition. Through professional pride, integrity, and teamwork, I shall be the example for all Marines to emulate."

—**Force Recon Creed**

►► WATER SURVIVAL COURSE

U.S. Marines usually operate either near, on, or in water, whether they are at sea, on rivers, or even in lakes and swamps.

Marines have to be comfortable in the water and must learn not to panic. All Marines take a Combat Water Survival Course, where they learn skills such as how to turn a backpack into a flotation device and how to swim with heavy equipment by making an unusual pedalling motion with their legs.

▼ **A Marine floats in full battledress and kit during an exercise in the swimming pool.**

 Newly qualified Marine officers swim in the pool as part of the Water Survival Training Program.

Abandon Ship

Marines also learn how to abandon ship. The training includes stepping off a 10-foot (3-meter) tower and dropping into a pool with legs crossed and arms crossed over the chest. Recruits also have to swim 80 ft (25 m) in uniform and boots. They must also be able to remove their flak jackets and helmets underwater in ten seconds.

Helicopter Crashes

When helicopters crash in water, they often flip upside down. This disorients the occupants more than the shock of the crash. Marines learn to escape from a spinning simulator, and how to follow their own air bubbles to the surface.

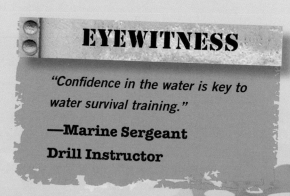

EYEWITNESS

"Confidence in the water is key to water survival training."

—Marine Sergeant Drill Instructor

VISIT, BOARD, SEARCH, AND SEIZURE

Visit, Board, Search, and Seizure (VBSS) is the most important tactic used by Marines when they have to intercept vessels suspected of piracy or smuggling.

Some VBSS operations are relatively straightforward. The target vessel agrees to being boarded and searched. At other times, ships try to escape or the crew actively tries to prevent the Marines boarding. When the ship's deck is high above the waterline, this is a dangerous situation for boarding forces.

Going Aboard
Marine Special Operations Battalions are trained to board

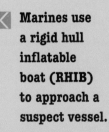

Marines use a rigid hull inflatable boat (RHIB) to approach a suspect vessel.

ships either by fast-roping from a helicopter or by climbing on board from a rigid hull inflatable boat (RHIB). The Marines are trained in offensive boarding, when they bring the crew under fire, and in defensive boarding, where they have to protect themselves from gunfire from the ship.

Search Skills

Once they are onboard and the crew's opposition has been overcome, Marines are trained to use explosives or metal-cutting equipment to find any secret compartments in a ship, and to inspect its cargo.

 U.S. Marines keep their rifles at the ready as their colleagues climb the side of a ship during a VBSS exercise.

EYEWITNESS

"Whether in support of the counter-narcotics mission or our new, more aggressive approach to stopping piracy, extensive training and the teamwork and principles of risk management that it has instilled has resulted in safe mission accomplishment."

—U.S. Navy Commander

ROTARY-WING AND TILT-ROTOR PILOT

The U.S. Marine Corps has its own air wing. That means it needs skilled pilots to fly its ship- and shore-based rotary-wing (helicopters) and tiltrotor aircraft.

Pilots have the longest training of any Marines. It includes a six-week preliminary course, a twenty-two-week course in Primary Flight Training, and between twenty-seven and forty-four weeks of Advanced Flight Training.

Marine pilots land an MV-22B Osprey tilt-rotor on the flight deck of the aircraft carrier USS *Essex*.

Special Roles

Once they have qualified, pilots choose whether they want to fly helicopters or tilt-rotor aircraft. They can also choose the size and type of aircraft, which influences their role. Within the Marine Air-Ground Task Force (MAGTF), for example, pilots may specialize in transporting Marines, ground attack, or casualty evacuation.

Forward Air Control

To communicate better with Marines on the ground, pilots undergo other training away from their aircraft. They learn how to work with the infantry or with an armored battalion as a Forward Air Controller, directing aircraft

Marines freefall from the rear door of an Osprey tilt-rotor.

to attack enemy targets. The experience is useful when they return to their squadrons. It gives them a better appreciation of the challenges faced by the infantry on the ground.

EYEWITNESS

"You incorporate all aspects of aviation in one air frame ... We do a spiral dive and, as we are coming down, we convert into a helicopter so we can bring the aircraft down and land."

—U.S. Marine Corps tiltrotor MV-22 Osprey pilot

⯈⯈ AAV CREWMAN

The Marines are closely associated with the sea, and one of their key skills is making amphibious landings. For this, the infantry rely on the men who crew Amphibious Assault Vehicles (AAVs).

The Amphibious Assault Vehicle (AAV) is a development from the landing craft used by the Marines during World War II. Those flat-bottomed vessels were designed to ground themselves on beaches and to lower a front ramp to let the Marines out. Modern AAVs come ashore on the beaches—and just keep going. They are designed to handle equally well on land as at sea.

Tracked Vehicles

AAVs are tracked armored vehicles designed to carry twenty-four Marines or cargo into battle. The armor protects the Marines while the AAV

A crewman steers an AAV full of Marines toward a warship offshore.

 The crew of an AAV look out through their hatches during a training exercise.

approaches the shore at speeds of up to 10 knots (11.5 mph; 18.5 km/h). On land, it travels at up to 45 miles per hour (72 km/h).

Crewman Roles

AAV Marines complete an Assault Amphibian Crewman Course that prepares them for a variety of roles in amphibious operations:
• An AAV Rear Crewman oversees the embarkation and disembarkation of Marines and also controls the weapons station.
• An AAV driver controls the AAV on land and water.
• An AAV commander directs the overall mission.

EYEWITNESS

"From ship to shore to objective, no equipment better defines the distinction and purpose of Marine Corps expeditionary capabilities than the AAV-7 Amphibious Assault Vehicle."

—U.S. Marine Corps official brief

⟫ MOUNTAIN WARFARE TRAINING

Although Marines are mostly associated with water, they also operate in the mountains, as in Afghanistan in 2001 during Operation Enduring Freedom.

The Marines have their own Mountain Warfare Training Center at Pickel Meadows, California. It provides a range of courses in specialized skills and familiarizes Marines with the mountain environment.

Specialized Courses

Different courses include summer and winter mountain leaders' courses; the scout sniper's course, which focuses on mountain tactics and firing from high angles; the mountain communications course; the animal packing course, where they learn to load equipment onto

⟫ An instructor watches a Marine recruit rappel down a wall, an essential climbing skill.

a horse; and the horsemanship course. Horses were indispensable in Afghanistan. Special forces there used horses while working with local fighters against the Taliban in regions that would have been inaccessible by vehicle.

Mountain Survival

Marines also undergo a mountain survival course. It teaches them how to find their way out of the mountains or how best to await rescue, even if they have lost all of their equipment and supplies.

 Marine Mountain Warfare instructors reach the summit of Mount McKinley in Alaska in 2014.

IN ACTION

Horsemanship can be highly useful in warfare. Horses can cross any type of terrain, even in places that vehicles can't reach. Not only do they make a unit quicker and more mobile than traveling on foot, they also allow soldiers to leave the roads, so they can avoid roadside bombs or ambushes.

They learn to build fires and shelters, find water, and navigate their way to safety. Lack of shelter and changing weather make moutains challenging places in which to survive.

▶▶ AIRCRAFT

The U.S. Marines use a full range of aircraft. Having their own combat air wing means the Marines can go to war without needing support from any other branch of the military.

One of the key roles of Marine aircraft is ground support. Both fighter aircraft and helicopter gunships use their guns to target enemy troops during a Marine assault.

A Marine F-35 Lightning II flies a patrol above a naval air station in Maryland in 2011.

The F-35 Lightning II is a cutting-edge fighter aircraft that uses stealth technology to shield it from enemy radar. It is capable of Short Take

 Marines prepare to hook a heavy howitzer to the bottom of a Super Stallion helicopter.

Off and Vertical Landing (STOVL), which means that it can be used for operations from land bases or aircraft carriers.

Super Stallion

The CH53E Super Stallion is a heavy-lift helicopter designed to transport heavy equipment to Marines in the front line. It can carry a light armored vehicle as well as thirty-seven combat-ready

Marines. Despite its size, the Super Stallion is also compact enough to be carried onboard amphibious assault ships.

IN ACTION

The V-22B Osprey is the most recent aircraft in the Marine armory—but it is already one of the most important. This tilt-rotor aircraft can take off and land vertically, like a helicopter. But it is quicker than a helicopter and can carry much larger loads.

►► WHEELED VEHICLES

What makes the U.S. Marines so effective as a fighting force is their mobility. A range of vehicles allows them to get into action quickly.

∨
∨ **The LAV-25 can be driven in four- or eight-wheel drive according to the roughness of the terrain.**

The LAV-25 is a light armored vehicle used in a range of roles, including command and control, reconnaissance, and assault. It can travel at 60 miles per hour (96 km/h) and is armed with a cannon and two machine guns.

AAV-7

The AAV-7 Amphibious Assault Vehicle is in some ways the essential Marine Corps vehicle. It provides the crossover from sea to land that is central to the Marine Corps' success.

The AAV-7 is designed to float out of the lower deck of a Navy assault ship and move quickly to land while providing protection for the Marines on board. The AAV crew can defend themselves with smoke and offensive grenade launchers and a .50-caliber machine gun mounted in the turret.

 The tracked AAV-7 makes an easy switch from amphibious to land operations.

IN ACTION

The Marines go into battle with all the equpiment they might need. That means they have heavy artillery, such as cannons and howitzers, and they also have their own tanks. Some of their hardware is bought from other armed forces and adapted.

RIFLES AND MACHINE GUNS

The Marines have a saying, "Every Marine a rifleman." From the early days of their training, Marines learn to rely on and care for their rifles.

One of the basic Marine rifles is the M4. This is a magazine-fed selective-fire light rifle that can provide rapid fire at close range. The M4 can also be adapted to carry a range of accessories mounted on rails on the top, including a close-combat optic sight, which projects a red dot of light onto a target.

A Marine provides covering fire with an M429 machine gun, a variant on the popular M420.

The M240 Machine Gun

The M240 provides heavy and precise fire at ranges of over 2 miles (3.2 km). It provides covering fire as Marines maneuver into position. The M240 can be carried by a squad of Marines or mounted on vehicles.

M110 Semiautomatic Sniper System

The Marine Scout Snipers have a legendary reputation. The M110 is one of their most adaptable weapons. It is capable of semiautomatic fire but can also fire accurate single shots at ranges of up to 2,625 feet (800 m).

 The M110 Semiautomatic Sniper System is capable of highly accurate single shots.

M240 MACHINE GUN
Ammunition: 7.62mm
Range: 1,800 meters effective/ 3,725 meters maximum
Weight: 24 pounds
Length: 47.5 inches

M110 SEMI-AUTOMATIC SNIPER SYSTEM (SASS)
Ammunition: 7.62mm
Range: 800 meters
Weight: 15.3 pounds
Length: 40.5 inches

▶▶ OVERTHROW OF THE TALIBAN, 2001

The U.S. Marine Corps played a key role in Operation Enduring Freedom in Afghanistan in 2001 and 2002. The operation overthrew the Taliban government and its al-Qaeda allies.

Al-Qaeda launched terrorist attacks on New York and Washington, D.C., on September 11, 2001. Within days, U.S. Marines were in Afghanistan. Its radical Islamic government, the Taliban, harbored al-Qaeda.

 Marines set out to secure the perimeter of a U.S. base in Afghanistan in 2001.

 A Marine keeps watch from a position defending a U.S. base.

First Operations

Working with both the U.S. Army and Special Forces, the Marines began to conduct operations in southern Afghanistan. Their role included supporting special forces during special reconnaissance missions, taking over Kandahar airport, and interrupting enemy lines of communication.

Big Impact

The Marines' rapid arrival had a significant impact at an early stage of the war. Having thought that they were safe in remote parts of Afghanistan, Taliban and al-Qaeda leaders found the U.S. Marines on their doorstep—and sometimes bursting through the door.

EYEWITNESS

"The Taliban likes to engage us, and I like to make it an unfair fight. If you shoot at us with 7.62 millimeter bullets, I'm going to respond with rockets."

—**Captain Chris Esrey, USMC, Sangin, 2010**

▶▶ OPERATION IRAQI FREEDOM

U.S. Marines were among the first forces to enter Iraq during the invasion of 2003. The following year, they were involved in ferocious street fighting.

 Marines prepare to clear a mosque during the fighting for Fallujah.

Fallujah was a key base for insurgents. These armed rebels resisted the occupation by using guerrilla warfare and

A Marine shouts to his unit during street fighting in Fallujah.

terrorist attacks. In late 2004, the U.S. Marines launched Operation Phantom Fury to drive the insurgents from the town.

The Battle Rages

The Marines and their British and Iraqi allies faced up to 4,000 dug-in insurgents. The town was full of booby traps—but the improvised explosive devices (IEDs) were no match for the Marine tanks that cleared the way for four battalions of infantry. The Marines finally cleared the town seven weeks later.

EYEWITNESS

"There's a lot of brave [Marines] there, and they took it in the face a lot of times, because they were doing it the old-fashioned way as infantrymen, and that's a hard business. I've got nothing but respect for those fellows."

—Major Tim Karcher, 7th Cavalry Regiment, Fallujah

GLOSSARY

amphibious Describes an operation that takes place on water and land.

covert Describes something that takes place secretly.

direct action Small-scale military operations that involve contact with the enemy.

ethos The characteristic spirit of a group of people.

expeditionary Describes a military force put together for an overseas mission.

foreign internal defense Military training for overseas forces so that they can better defend themselves.

guerrillas Small groups of fighters who use irregular tactics, such as ambushes and terrorism.

infiltrate To move into position for an operation without being spotted by the enemy.

insurgents Rebels fighting against a government or an invasion force.

intelligence Information about enemy troops and plans.

logistics The organization of troop movements and supplies.

martial arts Various techniques for unarmed combat.

poolee A newly recruited Marine who is still training.

rappel To slide quickly down a rope.

reconnaissance To use observation to find out about an enemy's position.

scout A soldier who moves ahead of a main force to gather information about an area or about the enemy.

sniper A marksman who shoots at people from a hidden position.

stealth Describes technology used to disguise aircraft and vehicles to stop them being located by radar.

surveillance Close observation of the enemy.

tilt-rotor An aircraft that combines wings with rotors.

trajectory The path followed by a bullet or missile.

FURTHER INFORMATION

BOOKS

David, Jack. *United States Marine Corps.* Torque Books. Minneapolis, MN: Bellwether Media, 2008.

Goldish, Meish. *Marine Corps: Civilian to Marine.* Becoming a Soldier. New York, NY: Bearport Publishing, 2010.

Gordon, Nick. *Marine Corps Force Recon.* US Military. Minneapolis, MN: Bellwether Media, 2013.

Lusted, Marcia Amidon. *Marine Force Recon: Elite Operations.* Military Special Ops. Minneapolis, MN: Lerner Publications, 2013.

Montana, Jack. *Marines.* Special Forces: Protecting, Building, Teaching, and Fighting. Broomall, PA: Mason Crest Publishers, 2010.

Reed, Jennifer. *Marines of the U.S. Marine Corps.* People of the U.S. Armed Forces. North Mankato, MN: Pebble Plus, 2009.

Rudolph, Jennifer. *Marine Scout Snipers in Action.* Special Ops II. New York, NY: Bearport Publishing, 2013.

WEBSITES

www.marines.mil
The official website of the U.S. Marine Corps.

science.howstuffworks.com/marines.htm
How Stuff Works pages about the U.S. Marines.

marinesmagazine.dodlive.mil
The online edition of the Marines' magazine.

www.mcu.usmc.mil/historydivision/SitePages/Home.aspx
Pages on the history of the Marines from the Marine Corps site.

Publisher's note to educators and parents: Our editors have carefully reviewed these websites to ensure that they are suitable for students. Many websites change frequently, however, and we cannot guarantee that a site's future contents will continue to meet our high standards of quality and educational value. Be advised that students should be closely supervised whenever they access the Internet.

INDEX